AF730420

THE HIP-POCKET GUIDE TO TESTIFYING IN COURT

2ND EDITION

BY

MARC D. GARFINKLE, ESQ.

HIP-POCKET GUIDE PRESS, LLC

THE HIP-POCKET GUIDE TO TESTIFYING IN COURT

2ND EDITION

BY

MARC D. GARFINKLE, ESQ.

2070 Millburn Avenue
Maplewood, NJ 07040
973-275-1313

ISBN 978-09843801-6-9

Dedicated to the many teachers, lawyers and judges who strive to bring justice to the law, remedies to the wronged, and integrity to our system of jurisprudence.

Table of Contents

THE HIP-POCKET GUIDE TO TESTIFYING IN COURT

BY
MARC D. GARFINKLE, ESQ

So you're going to court . . .

Some in cashmere and some in chains, millions of Americans testify (give a sworn statement) in court every year. Some of those millions will be parties to civil cases ("lawsuits"); others will be defendants in criminal cases ("prosecutions"); still others will be "fact" or "expert" witnesses with knowledge or information about a case.

You may be in court to explain a creative left turn, to describe what you saw while looking out a window, or to clarify for a jury some matter requiring your particular expertise. You may be in court to ask for a divorce or a name change or a restraining order, or to fight for your liberty when accused of a crime.

You may spend less than two minutes standing behind a podium, or two weeks seated at counsel table. Whether you come to court as a party or as a "fact witness," in a civil case or criminal, with counsel or without, **this guide will help you to optimize your effectiveness when you testify.**

What follows is not legal advice, but **some suggestions from a trial lawyer as to how to do your best when testifying in court**. They are based on experience, observation and common sense.

If you have a lawyer, and her advice differs from that given here, listen to your lawyer. She should know best. Each case is unique; each judge is individual; and legal customs and practices vary widely. In view of this, the advice that follows, while universal, is also general. Be guided accordingly.

<u>I have nothing to wear. . .</u>

Seemingly every courthouse contains an image of blind Justice - stately, balance in hand. Her blindfold symbolizes that justice will not be influenced by one's position in life, politics, color or fashion sense. Justice belongs equally to the shabbily dressed and the sharply attired.

Indeed, many courts allow witnesses and litigants to be dressed in the most casual wear. T-shirts, jeans, sneakers, tank tops, sweat pants and even shorts are increasingly in evidence in the courts. Rare is the judge who sends a person home for dirty or inappropriate clothing.

This is to your advantage. You have an early opportunity to distinguish yourself favorably by dressing correctly. In some courts, especially urban ones, you may be the only nicely dressed "civilian" in court. You may be even mistaken for a lawyer. But you will testify better when you dress properly for court. Proper dress? The rule is simple: **Dress as the judge would dress if he were in your shoes.**

For men, a suit or jacket and tie is usually appropriate. Women should wear dresses or skirt suits or business attire. (While pantsuits seem perfect, some courts still disapprove of them - you may wish to check with a local attorney or the court clerk.)

Men should avoid showy jewelry, heavy gold chains and pinky rings. They echo negative stereotypes. They should remove their hats upon entering the courthouse. Shoes should be polished. Sneakers are out, except for seniors.

Women might want wear modest earrings or a necklace or bracelet, but jewelry should be de-emphasized. Some courts allow women to keep their hats on; others do not. Hats should be simple, discrete, and easily removed without upsetting the coiffure.

If you are appearing in federal court, the dress is more formal, as are the demeanor of the court and counsel, as a rule. The courtrooms are generally impressive, and the judges are less tolerant of breaches in decorum or attacks on the formality and solemnity of the proceeding than the average judge in a lower court.

If you are appearing in mediation, arbitration, workers' compensation court or before a board or commission, you may find that the dress code is more relaxed. If unsure, err on the side of caution.

Your dress may be stylish, but should be modest and reserved. Sandals and sunglasses are out (even in Florida), and jewelry should be removed from facial piercings. Tattoos should not be flaunted.

Sexy or revealing clothing, however inappropriate, should *not* be removed in court.

I swear to God. . .

As soon as human society started to require testimony from its members, the need arose to insure the speaker's truthfulness. Of this need was born the ancient custom of oath-taking, or swearing to tell the truth. In antiquity, oaths were effective, because gods would strike dead anyone falsely swearing in their name. It's a fact.

Our modern oath works a bit like that, too. Once you are sworn, you are subject to punishment for any statement you know to be false. Lying under oath is called perjury. It should be avoided without exception. Perjury can also amount to contempt of court. Both offenses are crimes, punishable by incarceration.

Swearing is universal. Whether you are standing before a judge, seated at a deposition, pleading in front of the local planning board, or providing testimony to the U.S. Senate, you will be *"sworn," "sworn in,"* or *"put under oath,"* depending on local parlance. Usually, this means that you will be shown a Bible and asked to place your left hand thereon and to raise your right. When asked to do so, reflect for a second, as nervous witnesses often raise the left.

If you don't believe in God, or if you don't swear (for religious or other reasons), you have the right to affirm, or give an affirmation, that you will tell the truth. This just means that the swearing official (usually a court officer or clerk) will ask you if you affirm, rather than swear, that your testimony will be true. Some courts forget to offer this option; don't fret - you may feel free to tell the judge or official, *"I will affirm."* Certain religions prohibit testifying against another person in any circumstances. If you subscribe to such a faith, tell your attorney or the judge at the earliest moment.

The Perjury Dilemma. . .

The concept of perjury raises an interesting dilemma: since opposing sides of a lawsuit or prosecution cannot possibly *both* be right, then must not at least one person be committing perjury in almost every case? Couldn't every driver who loses on his claim that he had the green light, and every convicted defendant who had sworn, *"I didn't do it"* later be charged with perjury for lying under oath?

And what of the witnesses who have said, *"I don't know"* or *"I don't remember,"* when, in fact, they did? Makes testifying sound like a risky business.

It really isn't so treacherous. While every witness has the right to be mistaken (*"The burglar was about 5'8"*), she may not knowingly perpetrate a falsehood (*"That's not my signature"*) or otherwise fail to answer truthfully. Still, the line between perjured and erroneous testimony is often not clear. Fortunately, prosecution of perjury is relatively rare, as prosecutorial discretion usually filters out all but the most egregious instances.

In this vein, ethical criminal defense attorneys won't let a defendant testify to deny her guilt once she has told the attorney she is guilty. The *attorney*, who is not under oath, may still suggest to a jury that there is a reasonable doubt of guilt (and, therefore his client is not guilty). But if the defendant has already admitted her guilt to the lawyer, the lawyer will not let her take the stand and deny her guilt.

To do so would be a crime called suborning perjury, which is, in essence, encouraging perjury. Like with perjury itself, this rule seems to be frequently violated, and the offenders are rarely pursued.

If the truth hurts. . . plead the 5th

Sometimes an honest answer can get us in trouble. The wrong honest answer under oath can be costly, indeed. That's why the Fifth Amendment to the U.S. Constitution lets us refuse to give incriminating evidence against ourselves. This is our sacred right against self-incrimination - television's famous *"Right to Remain Silent."* It is one of your "Miranda" rights that ensure your fair treatment by the police if you are ever arrested for a crime. It is a supremely important right. Do not forget about it.

Generally, **do not say under oath anything that might be an admission to an illegal act**. Whether in a civil or a criminal forum, if you admit under oath to an illegal act or knowledge of a crime, you may trigger a prosecution or a lawsuit. Ironically, the most damning evidence against you might well be your own sworn statement. If you have any question at all that your testimony might get you in trouble, talk to a lawyer - *your own lawyer* - before you testify.

And nothing but the truth. . .

You want to tell the truth. But what is the truth? And, in particular, what is the *"truth, the whole truth, and nothing but the truth. . ."* Just how much information must you give? Must you state everything you know on the subject? The rule is vague: on the one hand, **you must answer directly and completely the question as posed**. Nothing more. On the other hand, you may not avoid giving information that was clearly within the contemplation of the question.

One guideline is that any question answerable by "yes" or "no" should have "yes" or "no" as the answer. For example, if you are asked, "Do *you remember what day of the week it was?"* and you remember it was a Thursday, then the appropriate answer is, *"Yes."*

That's it. *"Thursday"* will probably be the answer to the next question. The answer is not: *"Yes, it was a Thursday, which I remember because I had just dropped my mother-in-law off at her dentist's, and even though he's always closed on Thursday, my mother-in-law saw him on Thursdays because he was married, and they were having an affair."*

Such extraneous information will only give your interrogator more things to ask you, and may prove harmful to your testimony. Just answer the question.

Some questions defy the "yes/no" guideline. The all-encompassing question is one such. If asked, *"Was your car new or used?"* or, *"Were you at home or away?"* you should not say, *"Yes."* Be a bit more helpful.

You may find that a question seems

to ask for a "yes" or "no" answer, but you just cannot answer it that way. In such a case, you may say something like, *"At what point in time?"* or *"That depends on who is in charge"* or *"I can't answer that yes or no"* or *"It's not that simple."* When you finally give your explanation, remember to limit your answer to the question asked.

Sometimes on cross-examination your questioner will let you finish your answer and then wait for you to continue. Think twice before you volunteer more information. Don't get drawn into talking too much.

Le Grand Fromage

Most cases will be decided by, or influenced by, the judge. Most judges are lawyers or former lawyers who aspired to "the Bench" for many different reasons. Whatever their background, they are no longer true mortals once elevated to the bench. Learn the few rules that pertain to judges, and you will be happier for it.

Most importantly, **always stand when speaking to the judge and when addressed by the judge**. Similarly, stand whenever the court rises to leave or resume the bench. In most courts, the court officer will advise you to *"All please rise"* or *"Remain seated,"* usually according to the preference of the judge.

Judges should be spoken to with greater than ordinary respect. Although it is not impolite for a lay person to refer to a judge as *"Ma'am"* or *"Sir,"* it is much better form to call the judge, *"Your Honor."*

One should never say *"you"* or *"your"* when referring to the judge in court. It is better to say, *"Your Honor's"* or, *"the Court"* or even *"the Bench."* Formal speech enhances the solemnity of the courtroom. Regrettably, even attorneys have become more casual in speaking to the court.

For example, you may hear attorneys call the judge *"Judge"* while he's on the bench. This is informal; that moniker should be reserved for chambers (the judge's private office) or social settings, or when you bump into him in the hall. In court, if you say, *"Your Honor"* whenever you speak to the judge, you won't go wrong.

Irrespective of their myriad differences, judges appreciate witnesses who dress appropriately, arrive on time, listen well, speak clearly and answer directly. Be such a witness.

Hear ye, hear ye. . .

A big part of being a good witness is the ability to listen carefully. Equally important is the ability to be heard. If there are noises or distractions in the courtroom or the hallway that make it difficult for you to hear or be heard, you should tell the judge. Judges try to make sure that witnesses are audible, so that the court's stenographer or recording system will provide a clear record of all spoken testimony and colloquy (unsworn remarks of court and counsel).

When a question is asked, listen carefully to the language; reflect for a moment if you need to, then answer the exact question. If you think that you might not have understood a question or instruction, ask that it be rephrased or repeated. If there is a word you don't understand, say so.

If you need a foreign language interpreter, you may ask for that, but this is better done in advance. Do not begin to respond to a question or direction unless you are sure you understand what is being asked. To do otherwise is certain trouble.

It is also important to **wait until the questioner has finished her question** before you begin your response. Even though you think you know where the question is leading, allow it to be fully posed, and then wait a second or two before responding. This serves you three ways. It assures that you will hear the entire question; it prevents two people from talking at once (which can foul the record of the proceeding); and it provides you additional time to reflect upon the question and your answer.

Your answer may be limited by the question itself. Listen carefully to the question. Limitations such as, *"At any time prior to your calling the police,"* or *"Other than what you've already mentioned,"* or *"Since Christmas,"* may appear at the beginning, in the middle, or at the end of a question. Let them serve as the frames for your answer. That's why they're there. Almost every case features a witness who answers a question without heeding the limitations. Careful listening will help you provide accurate and unconfused testimony.

Another reason to listen carefully is to see if the questioner is asking you for more than the question appears to ask for. If you are testifying on **direct examination**, that is, you are a witness for the side whose attorney is asking the questions, the attorney may not word the question in such a way as to suggest the "correct" answer. Such a question is called a **leading question**, and is generally permissible only on cross-examination.

On **cross-examination**, an attorney may ask, *"Isn't it true that. . .?"* or *"That's why you killed her, right?"* or *" And only after he complained, you called the police!"* Those are all leading questions. An attorney who is trying to suggest the answer on direct examination will be much more subtle, so listen carefully to what is asked.

Actions speak louder. . .

We all know a bit about "**body language**". Psychologists say that a person's attitudes, confidence, and intentions may be revealed by his or her posture, mannerisms and gestures. Consciously or not, accurately or not, others read your body language to gain insights into your character or behavior.

When you testify, your body language comes under even greater scrutiny as judges and jury seek to learn all they can about you during your limited appearance.

Generally, we associate loose, easy, expansive gestures with truthfulness. Hands open, shoulders back. We associate tight, restricted or measured movements with defensiveness or uncertainty. Hands clenched, shoulders hunched, brow furrowed. Liar, liar...

To facilitate the body language of credibility, you should make yourself as comfortable as possible. It may help to eat lightly before your appearance. Wear comfortable clothing. Try to use the toilet, to stretch a few muscle groups and to breathe deeply several times before you testify. Voiding and stretching will help to make you comfortable and will improve your body language. If you're still nervous, that's okay. Few people testify without some butterflies.

Even if you have to sit on your hands, **keep your hands away from your face**. A hand near one's face is almost always bad body language. With rare exception, the person who rests his chin in his hands, or who twists her moustache, or otherwise speaks with hands partially obscuring mouth or face is not telling the whole truth.

Psychologists tell us that people who speak without moving their lips and people who speak through clenched teeth are harder for us to believe. In fact, the expression "lying through his teeth" suggests someone speaking through clenched teeth, as if to hide the source of the words.

Windows of the soul. . .

You may be standing at a microphone in front of a row of pews, or seated five steps up, in an enclosure alongside the judge. The jury may be a few short feet from you or yards away, across the room. Your questioner may be catty-corner from the jury or "in your face." The judge may actually be behind you. To whom do you direct your attention? First, look at the person who is asking the question. Then, let whoever will be judging you see your eyes as you respond. For this reason it is sometimes wise to remove your glasses or wear contact lenses while testifying, if you can do so comfortably and without squinting. As a general rule, **don't look *down* while testifying**, unless you're reading or looking at notes. Looking down is evasive and defensive. On the other hand, don't look up when trying to remember something.

Witnesses have an interesting manner of leaning back in their seats and rolling their eyes skyward when trying to remember. It's as if the answer is appearing on a teleprompter that is rolling across the backs of their brains. While this may be intended to suggest pensiveness and reflection before answering, it usually comes across as hokey or false

If you will be seated at counsel table or otherwise within view of the jury during a significant part of the proceeding, the judge or jury will be watching you with interest. It is important that your attention be unfailingly upon the proceedings. Try to never look bored (unless the other side's expert is testifying); you may smile, but try not to laugh at anyone's humor. Of course, if the judge makes a joke, you may laugh out loud.

<u>Just like in school. . .</u>

Be on time. Even if you *know* that court never starts on time, when told to appear at 9:00, do not be late. Murphy's Law has some courtroom corollaries. Believe me, you do not wish to run afoul of a judge who came in early that day to handle a particularly busy calendar.

Judges might not seem to mind keeping a courtroom waiting, but *your* delaying a judge should be avoided, if at all possible. It is a good idea to note and keep with you the telephone number of the court or the court's clerk. If you must be late, call the court. All judges appreciate the courtesy of the call.

Nervous habits can be distractive

and misleading. Avoid pencil-tapping, finger-drumming, knuckle-cracking, nail-biting, teeth-grinding, paper-shuffling, change-jingling and knee-bouncing. They all reveal that you're impatient or anxious. They suggest that you're not at ease with your surroundings. Chill.

Gum chewing is in a class by itself. Besides being disrespectful to the court, it obscures one's pronunciation and does little to enhance one's appearance of intelligence. Park your chewing gum at the door.

If, during the course of your testimony, you feel the need to use a toilet, tell the judge immediately. The judge will usually arrange a recess. Similarly, if you are thirsty, and a pitcher of water is not provided at the stand, you may request one. Many witnesses now bring their own bottled water with them to the stand when they testify.

Finally, if you should feel faint or ill, notify the court officer or judge at once.

It's better left unsaid. . .

When responding to a question, do not say anything that is not responsive to the question. This means: **do not volunteer details that have not been requested**.

It also means to avoid useless verbiage. When asked a question, do not mutter, comment on the question (*"That's a tough one."*), or say valueless words under oath. Try to eliminate expressions such as *"well," "ya know"* and *"all right,"* to introduce or interrupt a thought. Some witnesses say *"Okay!"* or *"Hmm, let me see..."* each time before answering; others repeat every question. If you must repeat a question aloud, don't make it a habit. Avoid gestures, shrugs and non-verbal vocalizations; a careful attorney will describe each for the record.

Don't say, *"uh-uh," "uh-huh"* or *"yeah"*. Don't state as your knowledge information that other people told you, unless you are asked specifically to do so. This could be hearsay. You may say what you heard, but make it clear that your information is not first hand.

People under oath seem fond of introductory phrases such as *"Honestly"*, *"To tell you the truth,"* and *"To be perfectly honest."* Such language suggests that your other testimony might be less than truthful. Avoid it. There may be times when you don't know the answer or perhaps you don't remember. You may certainly say, *"I don't know"* or *"I don't remember,"* provided that such a response is true.

Sometimes a witness is less than certain of something, but may be capable of providing a reliable estimate. During your testimony, you may be asked to estimate something to the best of your ability. In-court estimates usually involve distance, time, size, a person's age, frequency of events, or the speed of a car. If you believe that you can estimate (*"about 30 feet"* or *"from here to that clock"* or *"175 lbs."*), you may do so. If you cannot estimate, do not attempt to. And never, ever say, *"I guess" "I assume," "I suppose,"* or *"I imagine."* In the Midwest, however, one may *"reckon,"* if appropriate.

Three questions to expect

Generally, the questions will pertain to the subject matter of the case. Still, there are some lines of questioning, usually directed at the witness's credibility, that we have come to expect.

1. *Are you under the influence of any drug or medication?* Do not take offense at this one. No one is saying that your eyes are bloodshot; this is a fair way to

learn if there is some impairment to your ability to understand the proceedings or to tell the truth. If you answer in the affirmative, you may then expect a string of questions about your medication, dose, related side effects, and so on. If you must take a prescription drug, advise the court. It is not a good idea to take a sedative, except on doctor's orders, to control testimonial jitters. Such medications often affect your judgment, your reflexes, and your ability to stay awake.

2. *Have you ever been convicted of or pled guilty to a crime?* You must answer this one. Conviction of certain crimes can be harmful to one's credibility. A witness's credibility is always a potential issue in a case, and so your criminal record may become an issue, even though it has nothing to do with the case in which you testify.

Listen carefully to what is being asked. The question must be about convictions. Arrests, dismissals, indictments, conditional discharges and other criminal experiences may not be "discoverable" or usable in court. Some jurisdictions will allow disclosure of a criminal record only if the history shows a crime involving moral turpitude or a crime affecting truthfulness and credibility. Standards vary from state to state. If you are supposed to testify, and you have a criminal record, you might benefit from speaking to a lawyer before you testify.

3. *Did you discuss your testimony with anyone before being sworn in today?* This may hide a trap. He may even precede it by a remark such as, *"I noticed you standing in the hall talking to your company's lawyer during the last break... Did you discuss (etc.)"* The true

answer in most cases is, *"Of course, I did."*

However, the question may make the witness think that it may have been wrongful to discuss the case, and the nervous response is often, *"No."* The interrogator then proceeds to show how unbelievable that answer is. Most people have discussed the case with friends, family, fellow employees, attorneys and so on. There is usually nothing wrong with discussing the case, unless you're testifying under an order of silence (a "gag" order), or you've testified and are discussing your testimony with other witnesses.

Don't take the bait. . .

You may hear a witness for the other side make some outrageous remark...perhaps a blatant lie. You may hear a lawyer say something that is preposterous. **Do not react.** Do not stiffen your back in stunned disbelief, shake your head "no" with your brow scrunched, roll your eyes, hold your mouth agape or otherwise pantomime your shock or displeasure. No one will be impressed by the theatrics, and the judge has seen it all before.

Sometimes an attorney will ask the same or similar question over and over. Do not show your impatience or point out that the question is tiresome or repetitive. The attorney may be more interested in your reaction than in your response. Stay cool.

What does it all mean?

Being a good witness means testifying with credibility. It means being trustworthy and believable. Our credibility is the result of countless cues and signals we send. It is a reflection of our personal and cultural baggage. It is a function of our charisma, our physical features, and our world-views. It is tempered by our preparation for the task, our comfort level speaking in public, our health on a given day, and a hundred other factors. Some of these factors are within our ability to control; others are not.

Preparation and accurate information are important to good testimony, but confidence and sincerity are the essence. The most effective witnesses are those that are comfortable on the stand and at ease with their testimony. Experience will make you a better witness; the more often you testify, the better witness you will become. See you in court.

M.D.G.

About the Author

Marc Garfinkle is a New Jersey lawyer with thirty years of criminal and civil trial experience.

In addition to his practice, Marc is Adjunct Professor of Persuasion and Advocacy at Seton Hall University Law School and teaches skills for the National Institute of Trial Advocacy. Public Defender in Livingston, NJ, and former Chair of the N.J. Supreme Court District VB Attorney Ethics Committee, he lectures to lawyers, law students and police officers from coast to coast about trial advocacy and witness testimony.

The author of several books for attorneys, Marc is a member of Phi Beta Kappa, the National Association of Criminal Defense Lawyers, the American and New Jersey Bar Associations, the Association for Continuing Legal Education and the NJ Association for Justice.

Made in United States
Troutdale, OR
11/03/2026

56844883R00030